# Table of Contents

# Introduction

Hello there, are you one of the people worried about your bad credit score or even worse, those debts that you can't seem to get under CONTROL? Then this book was written for you! Do you want to raise your credit score and pay down or off that lingering debt? Again, this book is for you. Your time to stop running and hiding from creditors and start managing your financial obligations is now! You are finally about to read the book that will help you to change your financial situation and give you peace of mind. Now wouldn't you say that this is good news and a rare opportunity for you to find out how to make these changes happen?

Together, let's start to work on improving your credit score and eliminate your debts by following the proven steps listed inside. It will be our 'Your Self-Help Guide to Debt & Credit Management' to getting you back on a solid financial foundation. Your Self-Help Guide to Debt & Credit Management is a proven path with easy to follow steps that will take you through the process.

When I say proven path, it simply means that I have worked through my own report and debt management plan with these same steps I will outline for you. There are no long drawn out legal words or complex directions to follow. These are easy to follow steps that are understandable with suggestions that work. In fact, there are also charts, sample letters (that you can be tailored to your needs), and helpful information on your legal rights as a consumer.

Like many of you my credit score suffered as I kept putting off handling my financial obligations and neglected reviewing my credit reports. My debts kept creeping up and creditors were calling constantly, I became angry and fed up. I even tried contacting those debt repair services or debt consolidation firms but some of their solutions would have added more costs to my debt. Enough was enough and I sat down and began to put a plan together to resolve my financial issues my way. It worked so now I am offering my experience and tips from rebuilding my financial foundation and gaining peace of mind to you. I managed to get my credit reports updated, credit score improved dramatically, and debt management in control. You too can have the same success by following the steps in Your Self-Help Guide to Debt & Credit Management.

Now it will take determination, letter writing, consistency and hard work on your part to be successful. It is very important to stick with it and not be discouraged by any delays to your letters of inquiry. Your creditors want you to give up but don't you dare do it. You can repair your credit reports and pay down your debt, simply by following the steps in Your Self-Help Guide to Debt & Credit Management." Your efforts will bring you success and peace of mind.

We will begin with a little history and helpful information on credit bureaus and their importance in your financial management. There have been some changes to how credit scores are evaluated and bank lending and credit have tightened over the past few years. I have researched and included up-to-date information for some of these changes. I have referenced the sources and included a reference sheet at the end of the book. Now isn't it time that you get down to the business of managing your financial affairs? Remember, it will take time and work but the final outcome will be worth your efforts. Let's get started working with 'Your Self-Help Guide to Debt & Credit Management. I did it and I know you can too, Good Luck.

# Section 1--Getting to Know Your Credit Reporting Agency

Understanding how your credit reporting agency works is an important part of your self-help guide management process. Knowing how the credit bureaus operate will be a great help in communicating with them to get the services you request. There are three main credit bureaus: TransUnion, Experian, and Equifax. These are the three agencies that most creditors report to or go to, to view your information from other creditors. When you begin your SELF-HELP GUIDE project to improve your credit score, you will need to get a copy of your credit report from each of the above-mentioned credit bureaus. Why? Because each one will have different creditors information about your credit practices. Each company doesn't report to all three agencies, for instance, company A may report to two of them, one or all three; whereas, another company may only report to one of them. This is why you need all three credit bureaus report to compare with the others.

Credit bureaus do not share data; therefore, what shows up on one may not be seen on either of the other two. You must write to each of them so you can view your report to correct any errors on the report. If you write and ask for your free annual credit report by law they are obligated to send it to you. You can also call **877-322-8228** or go online to **annualcreditreport.com** to request a copy. In the next chapter there will be sample letters that you can write to each agency to get a copy of your credit report. You are entitled to one free copy each year so that you can review your report. If you have been denied credit by companies, you can, within 60 days of the denial letter, get a free copy of your report. The denial letter will show which reporting credit bureau sent information to the company. You must include a copy of the denial letter with your request to the credit bureau shown in the denial letter, so you will not be charged for the report.

Please understand that you have a right to complain or dispute any errors you see on your credit report. There is no cost for this service **DO NOT** let anyone try to charge you for this at the credit bureau. The credit bureau has a responsibility to investigate the inaccurate information and to correct it. Besides it's the law under the consumer credit protection act called the **Fair Credit Reporting Act (FCRA).** It mandates how information about consumers is gathered, used and shared. The FCRA also promotes the accuracy and privacy of any information in the files of consumer reporting agencies. You will be using this law by referencing it in your letters to your creditors. Your credit bureau and creditors will know you are serious and have some idea about consumer laws when you use the above act in your letters. Here are some of your major rights under the FCRA:

- You must be told if information in your file has been used against you.

- You have the right to know what is in your file.

- You have the right to ask for a credit score.

- You have the right to dispute incomplete or inaccurate information.

- Consumer reporting agencies must correct or delete inaccurate, incomplete, or unverifiable information.

- Consumer reporting agencies may not report outdated negative information.

- Access to your file is limited.

- You must give your consent for reports to be provided to employers.

- You may limit "prescreened" offers of credit and insurance you get based on information in your credit report.

- You may seek damages from violators.

- Identity theft victims and active duty military personnel have additional rights. (for more information visit

  www.consumerfinance.gov/learnmore

As reported on an Experian credit report (April 7, 2016), many states have their own consumer reporting laws and some will enforce the FCRA. For more information, contact your state or local consumer protection agency or your Attorney General. For more information about your federal rights, write to: **Consumer Financial Protection Bureau, 1700 G Street N.W., Washington, D.C. 20552.**

So don't be afraid to dispute any errors you find on your credit report. If you do not hear from the company, organization, etc. that reported the incorrect information and they do not respond within 30 days the credit bureau must remove the information. You will learn in the next chapter what information you will need to send with your dispute letter to have your account investigated. It would be a good idea to first try to get the information corrected or removed by writing directly to the company. See if they will contact the credit bureau and have the information updated or removed.

The credit bureau also must send a corrected credit report to you for free and send an updated credit report to any company that viewed your report in the past five to six months. The credit bureau can't list the disputed data on your report if the reporting company can't verify that it is correct. It is a good idea to keep copies of any letters of disputes, documents of proof, and all correspondence from both the credit bureaus and any companies you have written to. Also, be sure to review a copy of your credit reports semi-annually or annually for accuracy. Doing so will help you to catch any errors or accounts that may have been opened without your knowledge. Identity theft is on the rise and knowing what is in your credit reports may help prevent you from becoming a victim.

Bad credit decreases your buying power which puts a limit on what you can buy or borrow. Years ago a **FICO** credit score of **550-580** was considered a fair credit score. Today to have a good credit score you need to have a score of **640 – 850** and from **740** on to get good competitive interest rates. Please understand your credit score is different than your credit report. Your credit report contains your credit, debt collection accounts, charge-offs, and public records (i.e. bankruptcy, tax liens and court judgements), plus other information. The information in your credit reports is what is used to calculate your FICO Credit Score. Your credit scores is decided from these five factors: payment history (how you pay your bills, were they on-time or late, missed any, etc.); credit utilization (your debt to credit ratio); average credit age (how long the account has been opened); account mix (i.e. car loan, mortgage, installment loans, and credit cards); and inquires (the number of companies you have applied to for credit).

You can check your own credit score and it won't affect it, neither will a "soft inquiry" (promotional inquiries from companies who want to send you credit offers, insurance companies sending you information,). However, "hard inquiries" (you apply for credit or loan and the creditor pulls your credit). This may cause your score to take a small dip but is only temporary. Hard inquiries will drop off your credit report after they have been there for two years. These hard inquiries only affect your credit score for 12 months. The same applies to negative information; it usually "ages off" your credit report after a period of seven years. Chapter 13 Bankruptcy remains on the credit report for 7 years, Chapter 7 for 10 years. You will learn more about bankruptcies in a later chapter.

Usually the credit report shows the date the account is scheduled to be removed from the report. However, I have listed below how long some credit accounts stay on a person's credit report. The list is as follows:

- **Foreclosures** – they can remain on your credit reports for 7 years from the date it was filed. This also applies to a short sale may show up on your credit report as a settlement, a deed-in-lieu of foreclosure, settled for less than the full amount due or as a charge-off. These may be considered as derogatory events to some creditors viewing your credit report.

- **Charge-Offs** – Any account that you did pay as agreed (charged-off credit card or installment loan balance) can remain on your report up to 7 years from the date of the charge-off. Even if it is written off as an unpaid debt you may still owe the debt. Many creditors sell such accounts to collectors for pennies on the dollar allowing the collector to come after you for payment.

- **Late Payments** – They are reported on your credit report up to 7 years from when the delinquency happened. It usually shows how delinquent the late payments are such as; 30, 60, 90 or 120 days late. After the delinquency is 7 years old or after it legally can't be included in your credit history. Once the account shows closed the account can be removed from your credit report after 7 years.

- **Collection Accounts** – Collection accounts can remain on your credit report for 7 years plus 180 days from the date of the delinquency that preceded collection activity. Even if you paid the collection account, it can stay on your credit report for 7 years (plus 180 days) period. Some credit scoring models do not include collection accounts once they are paid.

- **Tax Liens** – The government could file a tax lien if you fail to pay your taxes. This will show creditors that the government has the right to take your property until you have paid or gotten a release of the lien. A tax lien can remain for 7 years on your credit report after the date the government filed the lien. You might be able to shorten this time span if you qualify for a lien withdrawal or the IRS Fresh Start program. Another option for you would be to apply for an Offer in Compromise or seek to put in the Uncollectible Status. You can learn how to apply on the IRS website and request the required forms needed.

- **Judgments** – A judgments time length depends on the state you live in as each sets its own limitation. However, most cases a paid or unpaid judgment can remain on your credit report 7 years from its filing date. Unpaid judgments can be renewed and could extend its life indefinitely on your credit reports. When someone renews a judgment filed the balance usually grows yearly. For instance: If the first filing was a judgment or $3,000 for an accident. You may have forgotten about it or was never notified. Yet it may appear on your driving record a few years down the line and the filer has renewed the judgment which is now $12,000. It happens to many people and affects your credit status and score.

Here are the general guidelines creditors and lenders use to determine if you are credit worthy and calculate score formula:

- **Payment History – 35%:** points out how you paid on your accounts and any late, missed or no payments are shown. Bankruptcies, foreclosures, judgments and wage garnishments which are forms of public records are part of your payment history. These can be serious negative marks against your credit.

- **Amount Owed – 30%:** This takes into account your available credit and your debt amount. It shows lenders you are more responsible in handling your credit's utilization. Having a lower balance is better than a high balance in any case.

- **Long Credit History – 15%:** having a long credit history shows you can handle your credit. Someone with accounts less than 3 months old or first timers have yet to prove they are responsible. One way to do this is to not close your credit card accounts but leave them open. It can build your credit score even though you're not using them over the years.

- **Types of Credit You Have – 10%:** it's best to have different types of credit accounts on your credit report. For instance: installment loans, mortgages, credit cards, auto loans, etc. Just having installment loans/credit cards and keeping them paid on time will help your credit score.

- **Inquiries/New Credit – 10%:** this is when you attempt to open new accounts or the creditor checks your credit report (hard inquiry). A soft inquiry is when you check your own credit data. Hard inquiries will cause your credit score to go down a little. When you do several inquiries like buying a car or house they are counted as one inquiry. This is considered a means of rate shopping as you decide on which car or house to buy (Richmond. March 6, 2015)

### Summing it Up for You

You just read about how the credit reporting agencies work. I'd like to sum up some of the information you should keep in mind. The three credit reporting agencies TransUnion, Experian and Equifax are usually the ones creditors and lenders report your data to. They are bound by the "Fair Credit Reporting Act" to investigate inaccurate information on your report. **You are entitled to a FREE copy of your credit report from each of the three agencies once a year.** You can also get a free copy of your reports within 60 days of being denied credit if you request it.

A few other reasons that you may want to check your credit reports would be the following:

- **Getting ready to move – not just mortgage companies check your credit reports. Now most landlords will pull your credit report before deciding to rent to you.**

- Applying for a personal/business loan – lenders want to be sure you are a responsible person that pays his or her bills and has the ability to pay them.

- Looking for a job – many employers that operate businesses handling money, etc. will most likely pull your credit report.  They will consider the debt amount and your payment history.  Probably assuming if you owe a lot of debt you may be a potential risks for mishandling money, etc.  Federal law prevents employers from asking to know or view your actual credit score.

- Looking for better insurance rates – many insurance companies use credit reports to determine your insurance rates.

- Better cable/phone packages – cable and phone companies view your credit report to determine the best package deals for you.  Your credit report could give them an idea if you can manage the added account.

- **Debt Collectors start calling – you will need to verify if they have the account and if it is an old account you can request they send proof it is your account, etc.**

- **Victim of identity theft – you may want to put a freeze on your account to prevent new accounts from being opened in your name if you feel someone has used your identity.**

- **Check credit reports regularly – pull each credit report 3 – 4 months apart to check for any suspicious accounts or errors.** It is a better way of keeping track of your reports.

Your credit score is determined by the FICO (Fair Isaac) system which starts at 350 (bad) and goes to 850, which is excellent. The Vantage Score 3.0 uses this same range. Both systems gets the information to determine what your credit score will be from your credit report. The scores offered now are based on the FICO Score 8 system. The earlier Vantage Score 2.0 used a letter grade to its credit score, depending on where it fell within the range. Example:

A = 901 – 990; B = 801 – 900; C = 701-800; D = 601-700; and F = 501-600 (High Risk).

Both the FICO and the Vantage Score credit scoring formulas mostly present the percentages for payment history and credit inquiries. Yet, there's a big difference in treatment toward utilization, age of credit history and types of credit. See chart below:

| CATEGORIES | FICO |
|---|---|
| Payment History | 35% |
| Level of Debt | 30% |
| Age of Credit History | 15% |
| Types of Credit | 10% |
| Credit Inquiries | 10% |

| CATEGORIES | VANTGAGE 3.0 |
|---|---|
| Payment History | 40% |
| Age and Type of Credit | 21% |
| Percent of Credit Used | 20% |
| Total Balances/Debt | 11% |
| Recent Credit Behavior and Inquiries | 5% |
| Available Credit | 3% |

| CATEGORIES | VANTAGE 2.0 |
|---|---|
| Payment History | 32% |
| Utilization | 23% |
| Balances | 15% |
| Depth of Credit | 13% |
| Recent Credit | 10% |
| Available Credit | 7% |

Now more lenders use the FICO score, checking this score may give you a better idea what your credit score is. Note the credit score you buy from the Internet won't match exactly the one the lender checks. It also costs to get your credit score from the credit reporting agencies; only your annual credit report is free. There have been some changes made to FICO 9 for which you should know. One change is how unpaid medical bills will be treated. Medical bills sent to collections will be treated differently than your other debts; they won't damage your credit as much as non-medical debts sent to collection. FICO realized through their research that unpaid medical bills were less of a credit risks than non-medical bills.

Medical debt is often shown to be out of the consumer's control. Another change is the treatment of paid collections. When your credit report shows a collection debt it hurts your credit score. The new FICO treatment will be to disregard any collection debts that the consumer has paid in full. A third change is how rent payments may count. Your rent payment history is included into the score, if and when a landlord reports the payments to a credit bureau. Consumers with a limited credit history this change will be very helpful to help them establish credit. In spite of these new changes many creditors are slow to change their underwriting process. Therefore, they favor using the earlier version, FICO 8 scoring formula.

## Section 2 -- Let's Get Started

The first thing you will need to do is get a copy of your credit report from each of the three agencies (TransUnion, Experian and Equifax). Here are their addresses:

- **TransUnion Consumer Relations, P.O. Box 2000, Chester, PA 19016-2000,**

- **Experian, P.O. Box 2002, Allen, TX 75013**

- **Equifax Information Services, LLC, PO Box 740241, Atlanta, GA 30374.**

You can also obtain a copy by going on to a computer to: www.annualcreditreport.com. You are entitled to a **FREE CREDIT REPORT** once a **YEAR** for your review. This gives you a chance to check over your report for accuracy and any errors. Please take advantage of this opportunity.

While waiting on your credit reports, gather up all your bills, collection letters, receipts, etc. So that you don't get confused, look at the dates on each document and receipt: those belonging to the same creditor and keep the most current one that shows your balance due. You can toss the others but if you are unsure of what to do with it hold on to it. Get a notebook or sheets of paper so that you can list each creditor, account number, amount owed, payment, interest, and due date. Create a table (or list) that shows all the above information. If you are familiar with Microsoft Excel putting this in a spreadsheet would be great. (See sample at end of section). Start with the largest bill due and work your way down from there. Be sure to match up any receipts, letters, etc. with the proper creditor. Once you have done this, look over all the accounts and decide which you feel should be paid off first. Usually the smallest is paid off first or the one with the highest interest rate. You can decide which method is beneficial to your financial situation. Then you can take that payment and add it to the next bill's payment to be paid off. This will allow you to pay off your bills faster. You can take a half payment of the bill you paid off if you will feel a money crunch. You will have a feeling of accomplishment with each bill paid off; as you begin to see progress with **YOUR BILL PAYMENT PLAN.**

Don't forget to try listing your spending pattern for a couple weeks showing what you spent your money on. I don't like to ask anyone to create a **BUDGET** for I find that people hardly stick to it. Heck, I never could but I do find it easier to keep track of how I spend my money daily. Once you see how much you are spending on items that you can do without; you'll be able to monitor your spending and put more toward paying off your **DEBT**. Create a new spending plan and make sure you allow for paying your utilities and rent, etc. Your bill payment plan will now be in place. (See example chart end of section) Now you are able to see your debt information more clearly and you can manage them more easily. However, you are not ready to send out letters to your creditors just yet. You need to have your **CREDIT REPORTS** back so you can review and compare to your credit list. Your credit report will show the following data for each creditor: **Name of Creditor/Account Number, address/PO Box (Maybe), Phone Number (Maybe), Date Account Opened, Date Closed, Date Paid, High Balance, Present Balance, Date Verified, Pay Status,**

**Account Type, Payment Terms, Remarks and Date Account Scheduled to be removed.**

When you receive your credit reports carefully check over the data shown on each. If you find anything that is incorrect you have a right to dispute it and to request that corrections be made. You can do this by writing to the credit reporting agencies directly. (See Sample Dispute Letter, end of Section). Send document or receipt that will prove your dispute. You may need to send copy of your photo ID as well. Check to make sure your personal information is correct on the reports too. You can request that only your last four digits of your social security number be shown on your credit report. Also, a partial Date-of-Birth (DOB) is shown. Otherwise, the credit report may show your entire social security number and birth date. Make sure your personal information is current and correct. Request they remove any additional phone numbers or employers, etc. Outdated personal information is confusing and unnecessary.

If any corrections or deletions are made to your credit reports, the credit reporting agency will send you an updated copy.

A letter usually accompanies the report to show what was investigated and changes made or not made and the reasons why. Recheck the credit report to be sure the changes were made and they are correct. After the credit agency verifies your information with the creditor and no changes are made to your requests you will have to contact the **CREDITOR** to have them change the data if you still feel it is **WRONG**. If a creditor has not responded to a request from the credit reporting agency within **30 days**, the agency should **REMOVE** their account from your report. There is a time limitation when a **NEGATIVE** account will be removed from your credit report usually **7** years.

Any hard inquiries by companies shown on your credit report are removed after **2** years so be sure to check the dates of any inquiry. If you see any listed after the 2 year period you can request to have them removed. When too many credit inquiries are showing on your credit report it lowers your credit score. Writing letters to agencies/creditors and receiving letters back takes time. Be patient. After a reasonable amount of time passes and you have not received an answer; **FOLLOW-UP** with a letter to make sure they got your first letter. **"DO NOT CALL THEM."**

Communicate with them by mail and keep a **COPY** of every

**LETTER** and **DOCUMENT** you send **OUT** and receive **BACK**.

If you are on the **PHONE** they can easily pressure you into

promising what they want and **NOT** what you can **DO** or **PAY**.

Plus, they can say they never got a **CALL** from you. Remember:

A **PAPER TRAIL** is your **PROOF OF CONTACT**!

It's time to send out letters to the three credit reporting

agencies to request your **FREE** annual reports. Create them on a

computer, if you can, it will be easier to go back to the letter. You

can change it if you need to write another letter. You can also

prepare letters for those creditors you wish to arrange payment

agreements with. However, these can wait until you receive your

credit reports back.

Another point, before you write letters to your creditors

check to see if the "Statute of Limitations" **(SOL)** has passed. In

the State of Illinois, the Statute of Limitations is **10** years for

written contracts; **5** years for oral agreements or contracts and **6**

years for promissory notes. You can do a search on the Internet for your state for information on their "Statutes of Limitations" (SOL).

Let me explain: Each state has a statute of limitations for when a

creditor can attempt to collect on a debt. If a debt collector calls or

writes you on a debt that has reached the SOL, you can write and

ask that they not contact you again. This letter is called a "**CEASE

AND DESIST**" letter. I will discuss this letter and others in more

detail in the section dealing with writing to creditors and debt

collectors. There will be samples of letters that I used which

proved to be effective.

## Summing It Up for You

This first section lets you know where to send your letters to request free copies of your credit reports. Remember you need to get a copy from each of the three credit reporting agencies (TransUnion, Experian and Equifax). I can never stress how important it is to keep track of what is on your credit reports. You want to make sure all the accounts and information listed on your credit report belongs to you. You wouldn't want someone else's bankruptcy to show up on your credit report. Such an error could cause a huge drop in your credit score; it could even signal that this error could mean identity theft.

If you notice any opened accounts on your credit report that you did not open, this could mean someone is using your identity. Checking your three credit reports regularly will help you detect such actions before they get out of control. Also, make sure all your personal identification is up-to-date. The correct information on your credit report can be matched to your identity. Remember your credit score will affect you for your entire life; it is worth the time to make any necessary improvements. It is never too late to start to build or rebuild your credit.

You need to focus on the five things lenders look for on your credit report; payment history, amount owed, length of credit history, types of credit, and inquires/new credit. These five things help determine your credit score. It takes time to build good credit, but it is worth it to be patient; use credit sparingly and make sure to make your payments on time. When you notice negative data on your credit report; check to see if the amount of its removal time is past. If it is you can request that it be removed from your credit report.

There is other information that you will learn about concerning your credit report as you read further along in my book. I can truthfully say that my experience with completing my debt management plan and credit report improvement; helped me learn a great deal about how credit works. Once I became fed up with creditors calling, letters in the mail, worrying how I'd pay a bill, I just sat down and decided I'd work on getting out of debt.

It took nearly three tries to fully and seriously stay committed to being debt and stress free. You can easily return to being overwhelmed with debt without realizing it happened. I'm human like everyone else and it took me some time to realize I had to take control of my debt and stay in control. Once I finally did that, I thought that I should write a book for others struggling with debt. Hoping my experiences with dealing with the credit reporting agencies, creditors, debt collectors, and the government could help others. It takes a lot of time and patience but with encouragement and knowhow, you can, get in control of your debt, improve your credit score and build a financial foundation.

## SAMPLE LETTERS TO CREDIT REPORT AGENCY

You can review the following pages for samples letters that you can review that can be sent to your credit agencies. If you don't have a computer or access to one to go online to request your annual credit report letter (**Sample Free Credit Report Letter**), your report can be sent.

Once you review your credit reports and find items that need correction or removal you can send a letter **Requesting Corrections**. See Section 2 where more about sending letters to creditors is discussed.

If you ever receive a "Denial Letter" from a creditor that turned you down for credit you can send this letter (**Due to Receipt of a Denial Letter**). You must include a copy of the denial letter with your letter. You have up to **60 days** after the date on the denial letter to request a **FREE COPY** of your credit report. This is another occasion that you can get a free copy of your credit report. However, you can only get it from the credit reporting agency that sent information to the creditor. The creditor will list

the agency and the reasons you were denied credit.

## SAMPLE FREE CREDIT REPORT REQUEST

## LETTER

[Date Here]

[Credit Agency Name]
[P.O. Box #]
[City, State, Zip Code]

Dear Consumer Relations:

I am sending this letter to request a copy of my credit report. It is my right to get a FREE copy of my report once a year. I have listed my information to assist you in locating my credit report:

  [Name}
  [Address, City, State, Zip Code]
  [SS #]

I hope the above information is sufficient for my request. I have also included a copy of my State ID or other photo ID for identification purposes.

Any further assistance you can give me in obtaining my credit report will be appreciated. Should you have any further questions you can reach me at; [Phone #]. I thank you in advance.

Sincerely,

[Signature Here]

Enclose: Photo ID

**(Send a Letter to Each Credit Reporting Agency)**

# SAMPLE FREE CREDIT REPORT REQUEST LETTER

## (Due to Receipt of a Denial Letter)

[Date Here]

[Credit Agency Name]
[P.O. Box #]
[City, State, Zip Code]

Dear Consumer Relations:

I am sending this letter to request a copy of my credit report. I have enclosed a copy of the "Denial Letter" I received from the company that denied me credit. I am sending in my request within the 60 day limit as required.

I want to review my report for accuracy and ensure the data listed is up-to-date. I would also like to request changes or removals of errors if necessary.

I would appreciate any assistance you can give me toward my letter of request. I, also, wish to thank you in advance.

Sincerely,

[Signature Here]

Enclose: Copy of the Denial Letter

**(You have 60 days after date of Denial to send this letter)**

# Section 3--Get Your Bills, Create Household Expense Sheets

While you are waiting on your credit reports, gather all your bills, collection letters, bill payment receipts, and any correspondence relating to your creditors. Get a sheet of paper so that you can create a list of each creditor with the account number, amount owed, monthly payment, date bill due and interest amount. Start with the largest bill amount due. (See sample at the end of this section). Place in front of you all your creditor bill information when creating debt management sheet. Be sure to match up all receipts, letters, etc. with the correct creditor. Once you have done this, look over all the accounts and decide which you feel should be paid off first. Usually the smallest bills are paid off first.

On your household income and expense sheet you will list your monthly income and what you spend on household expenses (i.e. mortgage/rent, utilities, food, phone, car payment, etc.). You will see all your household spending for the month on one sheet and your available income. The disposable income left will help you to determine how to manage your bill payment plan. It will also help you to see if your financial circumstances will allow you to have a debt payment plan; or if you will be better off filing **BANKRUPTCY!** Many people hate the sound of the word bankruptcy. However if your financial situation qualifies you for this alternative, then it is to your advantage to look into it. Note: your credit is already damaged so a listed bankruptcy will affect it for a year or two. **BANKRUPTCY** may carry a stigma because it remains on your credit report 7 to 10 years (depends on the filing status), but after a year you can rebuild your credit.

You are not ready to send out letters to your creditors just yet. You need to wait for your credit reports (three) to arrive. When your three credit reports arrive you will review the account data on the report. Then you will compare that data to the list of creditors you have on your debt management sheet. You will need to note the opening date of the account and the last reported information date from the creditor. If it is beyond the **Statute of Limitation (SOL)** you may want to request that it be removed from your credit report. There will be more on this when you begin to write letters to your creditors and to the credit agencies. Also, some accounts may not be on all three credit reports, as stated in Chapter 1. Some creditors don't report to all three credit agencies. Also, check the dates of any inquiries to your credit report; if they are over two years old you can ask that they be removed.

After checking and comparing your credit reports with your debt management sheet; you will be able to determine what letters you need to write. Some will go to the creditors and others to the credit reporting agencies. Your next step is to wait for answers from all the letters you have sent out. This is one of the main issues with repairing your credit reports and managing your debts, waiting for responses.

It is the main reason so many people fail to complete their SELF-HELP GUIDE plan. But if you are determined to get in control of your debt and update your credit reports you will have to spend some **TIME WAITING**. It will be worth it after all your hard work is done. It takes time to undo the damage to your credit report and score and to pay off your debt. Your credit report and credit score is a very important part of your financial plan(s).

Today, more than ever, a good credit report is necessary when seeking a mortgage, apartment, car loan, personal loans, educational loans and in some cases employment. Don't get discouraged and give up. It's a challenge but it is in your best interest to meet it and have a good credit report and debt-free life. Use your **TIME** wisely and work toward getting **CONTROL** of your **DEBT**!

Along with your household income/expense sheet; you may want to have a budget plan available. I particular didn't have a budget sheet but having one would make it easy for you to see what your money is spent on daily. This will enable you to see the areas where you may want to cut back on your spending. For example: maybe you've been spending quite a bit on coffee. Perhaps making your coffee at home and taking a cup with you will eliminate that cost for coffee. Cutting back on going out to eat during the week from 4 to 2 times a week is another way to save.

## Summing it Up for You

This section spoke to the need to wait for copies of each of your credit reports. Until then you must get your bills together, create a debt list and household income sheets. Samples of which will be shown at the end of this section. I provided tips on what to look for on your credit reports and to check your debt list to see how it compares to each of your credit reports. I stressed the importance of your credit score. Below is an explanation of how your credit score can go up:

- **Your Accounts Get Older:** the longer your credit history is the better your score could be. This takes into consideration how long your credit accounts have been opened, the age of your oldest account, the newest account and the average of all accounts (Brinkley-Badgett. March, 2016).

- **When Negative Accounts Age Off:** most negative accounts will age off your credit report after 7 years.

Collection accounts are 7 years plus 180 days from when it was first delinquent.

- **When a Creditor Increases Your Credit Limit:** credit scores are calculated by how much available credit is being used. So getting a higher credit limit is good as long as you don't start increasing your debt. You need to keep your debt utilization low.

- **When You Take Out a Loan:** it can help your score in the long run if it is a different type of account then any of the ones you already have. For instance you have credit cards and installment loans but you now take out a mortgage: your score may dip a bit due to the hard inquiry but the new line of credit will increase your score by show a diverse credit profile.

## SAMPLE CREDITOR DEBT LIST

Use this sheet to list all your debt accounts (credit cards, school loans, car loan, mortgage, payday loans, etc.).

| Account Name & Account Number | Amount Owed | Monthly Payment & Int. | Payment Due Date | Amount Paid | New Balance |
|---|---|---|---|---|---|
| Visa Card - 3200000345 | $875 | $15/21% | 12th | $25 | $850 |
|  |  |  |  |  |  |
|  |  |  |  |  |  |
|  |  |  |  |  |  |
|  |  |  |  |  |  |
|  |  |  |  |  |  |
|  |  |  |  |  |  |
|  |  |  |  |  |  |
|  |  |  |  |  |  |
|  |  |  |  |  |  |
|  |  |  |  |  |  |
|  |  |  |  |  |  |
| Total Debt: |  |  |  |  |  |

## SAMPLE HOUSEHOLD INCOME/EXPENSE SHEET

| | |
|---|---|
| **Income (After taxes)** | $ |
| **Other Income (SS, SSI, Alimony, etc.)** | $ |
| **Total Income:** | $ |
| **Mortgage/Rent** | $ |
| **Home/Renter's Insurance** | $ |
| **Utilities (Light/Gas)** | $ |
| **Cable/Internet** | $ |
| **Home/Cell Phone** | $ |
| **Car Payment/Insurance** | $ |
| **Transportation (Bus, Cab, etc.)** | $ |
| **Food** | $ |
| **Child Care** | $ |
| **Health/Dental Insurance** | $ |
| **Life Insurance** | $ |
| **Entertainment (Movies, Clubs, etc.)** | $ |
| **Total Expenses:** | $ |

**Income: $_____ - Expenses: $_____ =
Savings/Over Budget: $_____**

## Section 4--Compare Your Reports with Your Creditor's List

Now your work really begins with the return of ALL three credit reports. You will need to have on hand your creditor list and the three-credit reports (**Transunion, Experian and Equifax**). These are the three main credit reporting agencies you need to be concerned with. Let's take Transunion's credit report and begin to compare its data with your creditor list. First make sure that all your personal information is correct (i.e. name, address, phone, SS, work, and birthdate). If your entire social security number is showing, you don't want this on the report. You only need to have the last four digits showing. You can request to have this changed when you write your correction letter. Next check the companies listed in the hard inquiry section of the report (it is usually located at the end of the report). Check the date of the inquiry; if it is over two years old you can request that it be removed.

The time limit that a hard inquiry remains on your credit report is two years. Again, a **hard inquiry** is when a creditor has your permission to check your report when you are applying for credit. A **soft inquiry** is simply when companies are checking your credit standing to decide if they want to send offers to you. The hard inquiry is your main concern because too many of them will lower your credit score. It represents 10% of your credit score which is a low impact but you do not want to have too many inquires showing within a six month period. The effect of your credit score on your credit report is a temporary one. Another reason you want to have a higher credit score is that you will get better interest rates when applying for a mortgage or auto loan. Creditors view you as being a better risk because you are able to repay your debt. Having a low score, say below 580 could be a denial for credit. If you are given credit your interest rates on that credit would be very high.

Now we will look at the first creditor shown on the credit report list (usually the first section shows public record debts (**i.e. judgments, tax liens and bankruptcies**). You will notice it shows name and account number, address, phone number, when the case was filed, for the amount, pay status, last paid, on time/late payments and may show when the file is schedule to be removed from the report. You want to look at your creditor list and find the accounts you have listed. You also want to check for the last day the company reported to the agency, how much was paid, late payments, balance owed, and date the account was opened. The newer formats of the credit agency reports now show monthly payment amount, what amount was actually paid and missed payments. This gives a creditor viewing your credit report a more accurate account of how you pay your bills. If you find anything that is different on your credit report from your creditor's list make a note of it; especially if you notice any new accounts that are not yours. It could indicate that 'Identity Theft' may be at work. When you write your dispute letter you can request these accounts be removed. After you have compared each creditor on your list to each of the credit agency reports and made notations on the credit report, it's time to write your letters to the credit agency and if necessary to the creditor.

Note that you will need to once again put in **'WAIT TIME'** as you will need to give the credit agency and/or creditor time to respond to your letters. Remember that the credit agency has **30** days to investigate your dispute. If the information is verified by the creditor and is deemed correct it will remain on the credit report. If the company says the information is inaccurate and gives the credit agency the correct information; the credit agency must correct the file. If the creditor doesn't respond within the 30 days, the credit agency should remove the information. Once the investigation is done the credit agency will send you a letter with the corrected or deleted information shown. A copy of the corrected information in the credit report will be sent to show the new listing. You can ask that the corrected information be sent to any companies that have checked your credit report in the last two years if it was for employment reasons. Also, to anyone that received your report in the last six months.

Note that negative information or unsatisfactory accounts will stay on your credit reports for seven years. After that if they are still showing you can request that they are removed. The seven year mark starts on the date the account was opened. "There is no time limit for information reported in response to your application for a job that pays more than $75,000 a year or if you applied for more than $150,000 worth of credit or life insurance" (Ftc. 2013) The negative information will go away in time, in other words it will "age off." You can also reference the consumer credit protection law the "Fair Credit Reporting Act." It mandates how negative information is removed from your credit report and how credit bureaus are to act.

It is best to send typed letters in your own words or handwritten not a template used by everyone. You can perhaps get an idea of how to set up your letter, but putting it in your own words will get a better response. It is best to have a paper trail of all your correspondence with the credit agency. DO NOT CALL THEM because you will get the run around and may not get to the proper person to handle your dispute. They can also say they never got a call from you. Keep a copy of your letter as proof of your contact with the credit agency. Having proof of your dispute in writing will give you better protection by the consumer protection law. A sample of a template letter and idea of a letter in the sender's own words are shown on the next two pages of this section.

Your letter or letters may differ a depending on the corrections or deletions you request from the credit agency.

## Summing it Up for You

This section showed you how to compare your credit reports and what to look for. Also, compare your debit list with the data shown on your credit reports. If a debtor is not shown on either of your credit reports; it may have aged off the report (has pasted the 7 year limit). I gave you what to do if you find an error on your reports. You can dispute any errors you found by going to the website of the credit reporting agency. Here are their websites shown below:

**TransUnion** – www.transunion.com/disputeonline.

**Experian** – www.experian.com/dispute

**Equifax** – www.investigate.equifax.com

Using the Internet to start an on-line investigation will expedite the solutions to your errors. If you don't have access to a computer or feel comfortable using the Internet to request corrections to your credit report; you can mail them a letter:

**Transunion Consumer Relations**

WILLIAMS/DEBT & CREDIT/54

**P.O. Box 2000**

**Chester, PA 19016-2000**

**Equifax Information Services, LLC**

**PO Box 105285**

**Atlanta, GA 30348**

**Experian Consumer Relations**

**PO Box 9701**

**Allen, TX 75013**

It would help to have your file number to give them when disputing errors listed; it is located at the top right hand corner of your credit report. I informed you about what letters to write to the credit agency to request corrections to your credit report. On the next pages I have placed types of letters for you to review and send to the credit agencies. You may want to make some changes to the letters using your own words.

Remember be patient in waiting for a response back from the credit agency; they have 30 days to investigate your error disputes. Usually if you have provided the necessary information and documents (if any); the return response is on a timely basis. Keep all your correspondence to and from the credit agencies and creditors in a file for your records. This is very important and is your proof of communication with them.

## SAMPLE CREDIT REPORT REQUEST LETTER

### (Requesting Corrections)

[Date Here]

[Credit Agency Name]
[P.O. Box #]
[City, State, Zip Code]

Dear Consumer Relations:

I received my credit report and after careful review I found some items that need to be corrected or removed. I listed the information in error below:

- [Page #] Personal item [i.e. phone, address, employment, etc.]

- [Page#] [Account Name plus Account #] [List errors then the correct information to put in its place.]

Please verify and make the required corrections and forward me a corrected credit report per the Fair Credit Reporting Act requirement. Should you have any concerns or questions please feel free to contact me at: [Your Phone Number]. Thank you in advance for your assistance in this matter.

Sincerely,

[Signature Here]
Enclosure: Copy of receipts for paid off accounts, if needed

## SAMPLE CREDIT REPORT DISPUTE LETTER

### (Person's own words used)

August 11, 2016

TransUnion Consumer Relations
P.O. Box 2000
Chester, PA 19022-2000

RE: File Number: 00011000

Dear Consumer Relations:

I received my credit report today and found some items that need to be corrected. I have listed them below:

- **(Page 1) Telephone: 333-2222 is incorrect. Should read: 444-9999**

- **(Page 2) Adverse Accounts: Housing Mortgage #600000000****, Remarks: Chapter 7 Bankruptcy. Incorrect, should state that "Property Sold/Short Sale in Lieu of Mortgage.**

Please verify and make the required corrections and forward me a corrected credit report per the Fair Credit Reporting Act. Should you have any concerns or questions please feel free to contact me at: 000-0000. Thank you in advance.

Sincerely,

Carl Smith **(Note: all dates, figures, names and account #s used were fictitious.)**

## Section 5--Dealing with Your Creditors and Writing the Letters

Section four discussed the credit reports and comparing them to your creditor lists. This section we will spend some time dealing with your creditors. You should have reviewed your creditors list and now have some idea of what they reported to the credit agencies. If you have found any differences in the balances it is time to contact the creditors. First check your figure on your creditors list, find your last statement or correspondence from the creditor and write down the balance from the credit report.

It is up to you to determine how you want or plan to handle the debt with the creditor. A great deal will depend on the balance, interest rate on the account, date of last payment, and the date the account was opened.

*Why are these points important? First of all the balance will give you an idea of which bill you can easily pay off first. The interest rate will also help you to decide if you wish to pay off the lowest bill or the ones with the higher interest. The date of last payment will allow you to see the last time you paid on the account. Finally, the date the*

*account was open will determine if you will put the account*

*on hold (until you can make arrangements to pay it),*

*arrange a settlement to pay a percentage for the full amount*

*or refuse to pay because it is past the Statute of Limitations*

*(**SOL**). There is a different letter you would send to your*

*creditors for each of your choices. I will go into each of*

*them a bit more and explain how to deal with your creditor.*

*You can do this don't feel that all of the above is*

*intimidating. It is not, for the different way to deal with*

*your creditor depends on how you feel you can handle your*

*debt.*

Your creditor will try to persuade you to handle it his/her

way but don't fall for any scare tactics. You know your financial

situation better than your creditor, so who is better qualified to get

the creditor to accept your terms? You! It is up to you to inform

your creditor of how you plan to handle your debt. Once you

decide on the best way to deal with each creditor, you will send out

the appropriate letter and wait for their response.

Here again is that issue of **WAIT TIME**, I know we don't like it but, it is very important to have patience. Don't **RUSH** it. However, if after a couple weeks and you have not gotten a follow-up letter back respond with another letter of inquiry. **<u>DO NOT CALL THE CREDITOR</u>**! They will only try to pressure you into taking their offer or use threats to get you to back off your decision. Deal with your creditor via mail so you will have that "paper trail as proof of contact". This is why many of companies "record phone conversations from their clients" for their purposes. There are many companies that still do not provide such capabilities. Then the proof falls upon you to show you contacted them about your debt.

Let's say you happen to be in a position to set up a debt repayment plan for yourself. Which debt will you decide to pay off first? Will it be the ones with the smaller balance or the ones with the highest interest rates? Suppose you decide to pay off the smaller ones, good idea, as you pay off a bill you can take that payment and add with another small bill which will then pay that one off more quickly. Now if you want to pay off the bills with the higher interest rates most do once one is paid off, you will have

saved yourself a lot of interest. High interest can make a bill hang

around longer. Remember while paying off the higher interest bills

to be sure to at least pay the minimum payment on your other bills.

Whichever decision you make, make sure you can manage the

payments. You will feel good about your debt management plan as

you begin to pay off the bills one at a time. This will encourage

you to continue with your plan and not get discouraged. Watching

your debt amount decrease is a very good incentive to know that

what you are doing is working.

Knowing the last time you paid on a debt will give you an

idea of when you last interacted with that creditor. If it is a more

recent date you may want to continue making payments to stay in

good standing. You may also want to send a letter that puts the

account on hold until you can begin making payments again.

However, if the balance is low you may see if the creditor will

accept a settlement to pay in full at a reduced percentage amount.

When sending out this type of letter you need to have the

full settlement amount handy in case they accept it and you are prepared to pay it. Now if the creditor offers you a settlement amount to pay the account in full (at a percentage) and you accept; you still have an option to do so in payments. However, all creditors may not allow payment arrangements on a settlement but some will.

The fourth letter that you can send is when an account is (past the Statute of Limitations **(SOL)**. This is why you need to know the date the account was opened. This letter can be sent to the creditor (if they haven't turned it over to a collection agency) or to the collection agency the account has been sold to. The wording may differ somewhat depending on who you are writing it too.

There are statutes of limitations in all states where a creditor can <u>NOT</u> collect on a debt. I have put three state examples of their SOLs for your review. **(See Exhibit 1, Exhibit, 2 and Exhibit 3).** You can check the website www.statuteoflimitations.net to locate your states SOL listing. Once at the sight, you will click on any of the listed statutes (i.e. malpractice, debt collection, etc.) to see the 50 states.

Click on (more statute of limitations) for your state and the SOL chart will show. If you have a bill owed that is past this statutes time limit, **YOU CAN REFUSE TO PAY IT**. However, if you do get a legal notice on a debt you feel is too **OLD**, do not ignore it. Most **CREDITORS** hope you **DO NOT** show up in court so they can put a **JUDGMENT** against you for the amount owed. You definitely do not want this showing up on your credit report. Show up and bring proof the **SOL** has expired on the **OLD DEBT** in question. You can check with your state's "State Attorney General" to be sure there haven't been any changes to its **SOL**. Be sure that you have proof that the SOL has expired. Should a creditor or debt collector try to sue you over an **OLD** debt you can raise the statute of limitation as one of your defenses.

There is one more thing to consider when dealing with an **OLD DEBT**, if you pay even a small amount on the old debt, you can **RESTART** the statute of limitations. Then the **CREDITOR** can start collection or file a lawsuit for the entire amount you owe.

With regards to **OLD DEBTS** are you may want to try either sending a letter with a settlement offer or one saying you will pay when you are able. **Tip: DO NOT CALL YOUR CREDITOR** on an **OLD DEBT.** Should you happen to call the **CREDITOR** and are pressured into sending in just a small payment toward the bill and the (bill hasn't reached the **SOL** or you can't pay it in **FULL**) you have just made a bad situation worse.

Remember: to contact your **CREDIORS** via **MAIL.** Keep a COPY of all letters sent to your **CREDITORS** as proof of contact. Start to prepare your letters to send out now. A sample of an **SOL** letter and other letters for **CREDITORS** are at the end of this section. It is best to remember when dealing with your creditors or any debt collector, that you do so by letter. You will then have a paper trail of all your letters to and those from your creditors. Please be sure to have a correspondence file for each of your creditors; many will want PROOF! GOOD LUCK!

## Summing it Up for You

This section showed you how to handle different payment methods in dealing with your creditors. I used a mixture of each method and even took out debt consolidation loans. Here are some types of debt consolidation loans. See the explanations below:

**Debt Consolidation that Works:** you should use this debt consolidation loan to pay off all your other creditors. Placing your debts in a single loan will give you three benefits:

- **Lower interest rate:** lowering your interest will take years off your debt amount and save you a lot of money. You need to make sure your APR (annual percentage rate) is lower than on your present debts (Clements. March 2016).

- **Easier payments:** having a lot of bills to manage may be hard to do. While having one bill gives you one payment to pay. The idea is to have a lower interest rate and one low debt payment to make. Remember also, that a debt consolidation loan is not a method to allow you create more debt. You will defeat its purpose and put yourself in a far more dangerous position.

- **Higher credit score:** maxing out your credit cards will cause your utilization ratio to be very high. Such a high ratio will have a big and negative impact on your credit score. However, obtaining the debt consolidation loan and paying off your debt with it will reduce your utilization ratio, therefore; leading to an increase in your credit score within three months. Nevertheless, the better way to increase your credit score is to eliminate your debts all together this is why you are working on your financial management do-it-yourself plan.

People consolidate credit card debt to lower interest rates in the following ways:

- **Personal Loans:** it is slowly easier to obtain a personal loan with a low interest with some marketplace lenders. You should shop around online to compare the best interest rates that are offered. Some lenders offer interest rates as low as 4.74% (Clements. March 2016). Remember this depends on your credit score. A low credit score will cause a lender to charge a high interest rate that would make it better to avoid accepting the loan.

- **Credit Card Balance Transfers:** some credit card companies use teaser rates of 0% to try to get new customers. Now if you have very good to excellent credit scores and not a lot of debt this would be your cheapest option.

- **Home Equity Loans and Lines of Credit:** this is one of the most used methods of debt consolidation. The home equity loan has low interest rates and the ability to deduct the interest at tax time. The downfall is you are putting your home at risk. Choosing a credit union over a bank will give you lower interest rate; some loan equity loan interest rates as low as 3.74%.

- **Debt Management Programs to Avoid:** Debt management company advertisements are created to sound like debt consolidation loans. They are not and in fact will want you to pay them instead of your creditor companies. They will hold the money and will not pay your bills as quickly as you want them to.

Soon your accounts will start to become late, your credit score will take hits, and collection calls may start coming. These debt management companies will say they will try and negotiate settlements with your creditors for you. This may be happening as you are paying them to pay your creditors for you, but you are also paying them a monthly fee for their service. Plus some of these companies charge percentage of your total debt as payment in addition to the above. Now you are left to try and retrieve your money from the debt management company. Please do not get yourself caught up in this type of situation. There are legitimate non-profit consumer credit counselors that will help you to manage your debt.

## LETTER IN YOUR OWN WORDS WRITTEN TO CREDITOR

April 27, 2008


XZM Company

2222 Policy Drive

Somewhere, AZ 22233

RE:  Account #:  000-00000000

Dear Sir/Madam:

It is unfortunate that I must write this letter to you but I wanted to let you know my intention toward the above debt.  It is due to unforeseen circumstances I have come across that bring about this letter.  Therefore, I ask you to please stop communicating with me regarding the above account.

If you feel that you must turn my debt over to a debt collector, it is your choice.  However, I will hold them to the **Fair Debt Collections Practice Act (FDCPA)**.  I will take care of this debt when I am able to do so.  I have no garnish able income or assets.

I will contact you at a later time to make arrangements to pay this debt when I am financially ale.  Hopefully, at that time we can come to a mutual agreement to remedy this matter. I sincerely apologize for this delay in handling my obligation to you.

Sincerely,

Casual Smith
222 About St
Somewhere, TX 20000

## SAMPLE STATUTE OF LIMITATIONS (SOL) TO CREDITOR

[Date]

[Company Name]
0000 Nobody St
Wherever, OK 00000

RE: Account #: 00-00000-000

To Whom It May Concern:

I am writing this letter to you in response to the last letter I received from you on April 2, 1002 concerning the above account.

After careful review of this account I noticed that it is past the state's Statutes of Limitations. The type of debt and the date the account was opened has expired. Therefore, by law I don't have to pay the debt and you are to refrain from trying to collect this debt.

I'm serving notice that I don't want to be contacted about this debt anymore. I need to get a letter from you that states your efforts to collect on this debt will be terminated. I thank you in advance for your understanding in this matter.

Sincerely,


Casual Smith
222 About St
Somewhere, TX 20000

**(Note: If you would like confirmation that your creditor received your letter; send them by Certified Mail with return receipt requested).**

## SAMPLE SETTLEMENT REQUEST LETTER TO
## CREDITOR

[Date]

[Company Name]
0000 Nobody St
Wherever, OK 00000

RE:  Account #:  00-00000-000

To Whom It May Concern:

I'm writing this letter in regards to the balance on the outstanding account listed above.  I would like to try to work with you to settle this debt.  I am aware that your company has reported this account to the credit agencies which gives it a negative status.  If you are open to a request for a settlement so am I.

I am willing to pay $**** as settlement for the above account. If you wish to offer a counter amount I am open to it.  However, if you agree to my settlement amount, I will forward you a money order or certified check payable to your company.  In return, I would like a confirmation that the debt is paid per this agreement. Also, please confirm that you will notify the credit agencies you report to and have them update or remove my information.

I would appreciate any assistance you can give me and I look forward to your response by return mail.  Thanking you in advance.

Sincerely,


Casual Smith
222 About St
Somewhere, TX 20000 **(Note:   Send by Certified Mail with a return receipt requested)**

## EXHIBIT 1: ILLINOIS STATUTE OF LIMITATIONS

| | |
|---|---|
| breach of contract for sale | 4 years |
| defamation | 1 year |
| domestic judgments | 20 years |
| foreign judgments | same time as laws allowed in the foreign jurisdiction |
| injury to personal property | 5 years |
| legal malpractice | 2 years from date of discovery. maximum 6 years |
| libel | 1 year |
| medical malpractice | 2 years from date of discovery |
| municipalities | 1 year from wrongful death |
| negligence causing personal injury | 2 years |
| open accounts for debt collections | 5 years |
| oral agreements | 5 years |
| oral contracts | 5 years |
| personal injury actions | 2 years from date of injury |
| products liability | 2 years. maximum 8 years for injury or death |
| professional malpractice | 2 years from date of act giving rise to injury |
| promissory notes | 6 years |
| slander | 1 year |

| written contracts | 10 years |
|---|---|
| wrongful death | 2 years from date of death |

## EXHIBIT 2: INDIANA STATUTE OF LIMITATIONS

| | |
|---|---|
| asbestos and radiation related injuries | 2 years from date of discovery |
| breach of contract for sale under UCC | 4 years |
| judgments | 10 years unless renewed |
| medical malpractice | 2 years from date of injury |
| minors | begins on date of 18th birthday (except in cases of wrongful death) |
| negligence causing personal injury | 2 years from date of discovery |
| open accounts for debt collections | 6 years |
| oral agreements | 6 years |
| personal injury actions | 2 years from date of injury |
| products liability | 2 years from date of injury |
| promissory notes | 10 years |
| unwritten accounts or contracts | 6 years |
| written contracts | 10 years |
| wrongful death | 2 years from date of death |

## EXHIBIT 3: WISCONSIN STATUTE OF LIMITATIONS

| | |
|---|---|
| contracts | 6 years |
| defamation | 2 years |
| fraud | 6 years |
| injury to personal property | 6 years |
| intentional torts | 2 years |
| libel | 2 years |
| medical malpractice actions | 3 years from date of injury |
| medical malpractice action based on insertion of foreign object | 1 year after discovery of object |
| minors | 2 years after date of 18th birthday |
| negligence causing personal injury | 3 years from date of discovery |
| open account for debt collection | 6 years |
| oral agreements | 6 years |
| personal injury | 3 years |
| product liability | 3 years |
| promissory notes | 10 years |
| slander | 2 years |
| written contract | 6 years |
| wrongful death | 3 years from date of death |

## Section 6--Dealing with Debt Collectors

In this section I will give you some information about Debt Collectors, how the debt laws regulate them and the different letters you can send them to get them off your back. Some debt collectors can appear intimidating and do try to put fear into those they are trying to collect a debt. As with your creditors, DO NOT LET THEM pressure you into doing what they want; as they try to discourage you from your RIGHTS as a CONSUMER. Debt Collectors must comply with the **Fair Debt Collection Practice Act (FDCPA).** It's a Federal law that protects people who owe money and lets them know their rights they have and about what debt collectors can or can't do. One thing to remember is that any company collecting its **OWN DEBTS** is **NOT** covered by this law. It applies to a debt collector, debt collection agency or a collection lawyer whose job is to collect debts OWED to ANOTHER person. This Federal law **ONLY** covers debts for personal, family or household uses. Such debts as money owed for a medical bills, car, furniture, and credit cards.

I used to dread getting a call from a debt collector because so many were rude, pushy, inconsiderate and even threatening. Until I finally learned what they could and couldn't do and what I, as a consumer, could do. Whenever a debt collector calls you be sure to get information from him/her concerning the debt. Never state that it is your debt that wasn't paid instead don't discuss it on the phone. Have the debt collector send you information on the debt in writing letting you know; the amount of the debt; to whom the debt is owed; that they will believe the debt is yours, unless you dispute it within 30 days; lastly what you can do about it if you do not owe the debt. If you admit the debt is yours before verification, it could restart the statute of limitations. Find out if you are required to pay the debt if it is yours and if the statute of limitations has passed.

If you get a letter from a debt collector about an old debt they assume to be yours asking for a payment on the debt; DO NOT immediately send in even a small amount ($5, $10, etc.). Doing so would also be a way of restarting the statute of limitations and putting you in a position to be sued for the balance of the debt.

Debt collectors have ways of getting consumers to restart the

statute of limitations by unknowingly confirming an old debt.

Same applies to letters of a settlement for a percentage of the debt.

Don't agree to a settlement or payment plan unless you actually

owe the debt and it is not past the statute of limitations. It would be

better for you to send them a counter-offer letter of a payment plan

that you can keep up. Also, be sure you get a letter from them

accepting your payment plan. Upon receipt of their acceptance

letter, send the payment, by certified mail with a request for a

receipt. Also, make sure the debt collector has sent a letter in

writing that he/she agrees to remove the debt from the credit

reporting agencies.

At the end of this section will be sample letters that you can

change to fit your situation for Settlement of Debt, Validation of

Debt, and Cease and Desist. Never agree to an old debt, or sign

anything saying you'll pay a debt before you have checked to see if

it has passed the statute of limitations. You'll save yourself a lot of

stress and grief. If a debt collector says the debt is still active, you can verify it by, having a copy of your credit report to show the expiration of the debt. Your credit reports show your most recent data on each of your accounts. Remember you can get a free copy of each of your credit agency reports each year from Annual Credit Report **(www.annualcreditreport.com).**

Here is some other important information that you need to know concerning handling calls or mail from debt collectors. If a debt collector didn't prove that a debt was yours but continues to call you can request that they stop calling you. Hang up if he/she continues to call let them know you would rather communicate with them in writing. Or simply hang up. A debt collector is in violation of the FDCPA law. Therefore, if the debt collector keeps sending mail you will have proof of such harassment which may bring about a lawsuit in your favor. You can stop debt collectors from calling by sending them a "cease and desist" letter. Note: you can only send this type of letter to debt collectors NOT to the original creditor. When you send out the cease and desist letter to the debt collector or collection agency they can communicate with you one more time. They will let you know that they will no longer be contacting you or that they will be taking further actions. If the debt collector or collection agency contacts you more than the one time you will need proof of this. This is why you send any letters via certified mail requesting a receipt which would show that the letter was sent and received.

Another thing, when a debt collector makes calls to try to collect on a debt they can only call between the hours of **8:00 am and 9:00 pm.** A debt collector or collection agency **CANNOT** call other persons and tell them that you owe a debt. They can call them to find out where you live or work. They can call your lawyer, the creditor's attorney or creditor, credit reporting agency, parent (if a minor) or your spouse. Other illegal violations per the **FDCPA** that a debt collector or collection agency **CANNOT** do are:

- **Threaten you with violence.**

- **Use obscene language while talking to you.**

- **Constantly call to harass you.**

- **Misquote the amount of debt.**

- **Call outside the time guidelines; Threaten to sue,**

**garnish your wages, cause job loss, take your property or ruin your credit when he knows he is not going too.**

- **Fail to send a debt validation letter.**

- **Contact you at work knowing your boss doesn't approve; or use unfair means to collect a debt.**

Remember the **FDCPA** is the law that works for the rights of debtors (consumers) that have been harassed and mistreated by debt collectors. It informs debtors of what debt collectors and collection agencies **CAN** and **CANNOT** do. In summing it all up, you are right to want to know that you are paying the right party for an old debt. Sometimes the same debt is sold to several buyers and you may not know who is actually owed what. It is really important for you to know who owns the debt. You can verify the name of the company and the amount of the debt; you will find this shown next to the collection debt on your credit report. The original creditor of the account may give you the information as well.

You do not want to deal with bad or illegal collection agencies. There is no need to deal with an agency if the statute of limitations in your state has passed. Remember that a collection agency is in violation of the federal Fair Debt Collection Practices Act if they call harassing you or falsely threatening to arrest you. You can file a complaint to the Consumer Financial Protection Bureau (CFPB) if any collection agency does. The CFPB offers sample letters on their site www.consumerfinance.gov.

Here's another tip for those of you that have reverse mortgages. You are not obligated to pay it back unless you move, sell the house or dies. Anyone living in the house has to leave within six months should either of the above happens (includes relatives). You can ask for an extension if you want to try and sell the house or get a loan to pay off the mortgage. However, if the home's value is less than it is worth, you can do a "deed in lieu of foreclosure," which allows you to turn over the keys and walk away. What is good about this is you won't owe anything. A reverse mortgage is known as a non-recourse loan where a lender can't try to make you or your family pay the balance owed (Weston. March,

2016).

The following three pages contain samples of the letters to send to debt collectors or collection agencies as discussed earlier in this section. Good Luck on your way to financial stability and freedom from debt.

## Summing it Up for You

This section showed you how to communicate with debt collectors and how they should communicate with you. I also, informed you that debt collectors are regulated by debt laws as to what they can and cannot do. They can prove intimidating to some people and they will use it to try and force you into paying old debts.

There is no need to fear calls from debt collectors once you know how to deal with them. As a consumer your rights are protected by the Fair Credit Reporting Act. Debt collectors are regulated by the Fair Debt Collection Practice Act (**FDCPA**). Never assume because a debt collector is calling you that you owe the debt or if it is even yours. Question him/her to get more information concerning the debt. There is a letter of validation that you can send to a debt collector within 30 days of the call for proof you owe the debt.

Once you learn what collection agency owns the debt there are some ways you can take ACTION. This cannot be repeated enough to let consumers know they do have a way to fight back, please note:

**Validate the Debt** – a letter of validation requires the collection agency to provide you proof they own the debt and that you owe it.

**Dispute the Debt** – when you find out a debt is not yours is paid off, or time has passed, you may be able to dispute it. Review Section 4 for information disputing errors.

**Settle the Debt** – Should you decide to pay off the debt. You can discuss a deal with the collection agency on a payment plan. You can hurry the removal of a paid off collection if you request that the collection agency send a request to the credit reporting agency to remove the account. In time the collection account (if paid) will be ignored by some creditors.

**Consult with a Professional** – should you find dealing with the collection agency is time consuming or feel it is too overwhelming to handle by yourself. I found that true it is time consuming but the experience of doing it yourself will save you money. Yet you must do what you feel is best for you.

**However, be sure the professional(s) you choose are legitimate; many people have been scammed by those promising to help them.**

DO NOT say a debt is yours; DO NOT send any money on any debt (it could be past the Statute of Limitations) or sign any document saying you'll pay. Remember the rules and/or regulations shown in this section which lets you know when a debt collector is in violation of the **FDCPA**. This law works for you as a consumer (debtor) if a debt collector harasses or mistreats you. Again, know your **RIGHTS** as a consumer then use them to keep debt collectors in check. The next pages show the letters you can view and decide which will benefit you on your way to financial freedom from debt.

Here are some promising new rules being proposed by the Consumer Finance Protection Bureau (CFPB). CFPB says many consumers are wrongly being contacted by some collection agencies.

Most of the complaints they receive are from consumers concerning debts they didn't owe. Many are being harassed for non-owed debts, threatened legal action, calling them at work, even contacting their employers and giving out information to others. These new rules being proposed by the CFPB will focus on third-party debt collectors. (Picchi, July, 2016).

Under the new rules being proposed here are five things that third-party debt collectors will no longer be able to do:

- **File a lawsuit to collect a debt after the statute of limitations has expired.**

- **Demand repayment without informing a consumer of her/his rights.**

- **Incessantly call, leave voice mails or email to consumers – one major complaint from consumers.**

- **Bury a complaint by selling the debt to another collector – a new collector would have to investigate and resolve the dispute before trying to collect payment. (Picchi, July, 2016).**

WILLIAMS/DEBT & CREDIT/88

## SAMPLE DEBT COLLECTORS DEBT VALIDATION LETTER

[Date]


[Debt Collector's Name]
0000 Nobody St
Wherever, OK 00000

RE: Account #: 00-00000-000

Dear Manager:

I am responding to a letter you sent to me on <date>. I am not aware of such debt as belonging to me. I am requesting that you send me validation of this debt. I want to see proof that I owe the above debt before I make a decision that I have a responsibility to pay you.

As a consumer I have rights under the federal debt collection laws, to request the above debt validation letter. I am hoping that you will comply with my request Hopefully; there will be no further need for me to file a complaint with the Federal Trade Commission.

I am looking forward to a response to the above request via return mail. I thank you in advance for your cooperation.

Sincerely,


<Your Name>
<Address>
<City, State, Zip Code>

**(Note: Send this letter asking for a Debt Validation by Certified Mail with a return receipt requested)**

## SAMPLE DEBT COLLECTORS SETTLEMENT LETTER

[Date]

[Debt Collector's Name]

0000 Nobody St
Wherever, OK 00000
RE: Account #: 00-00000-000

Dear Manager:

I'm writing this letter in regards to the balance on the outstanding account listed above. I would like to try to work with you to settle this debt. I am aware that your company has reported this account to the credit agencies which gives it a negative status. If you are open to a request for a settlement so am I.

I am willing to pay $**** as settlement for the above account. However, if you agree to my settlement amount, I will forward you a money order or certified check payable to your company. In return, I would like a confirmation that the debt is paid in full per this agreement. Also, please notify the credit agencies you report to and have my information updated or removed.

I would appreciate any assistance you can give me in handling this account. I will look for your response by return mail. Thanking you in advance.

Sincerely,


Casual Smith
222 About St
Somewhere, TX 20000

**(Note: Send this letter asking for a Settlement of the Debt by Certified Mail with a return receipt requested)**

WILLIAMS/DEBT & CREDIT/90

## SAMPLE DEBT COLLECTOR'S CEASE AND DESIST LETTER

[Date]

[Debt Collector's Name]
0000 Somebody St
Whatever, AZ 10200

RE:  Account #:  00-00000-000

Dear Manager:

I am writing this according to my rights under federal debt collection laws to request that you cease and desist any further communications with me concerning all other alleged debts you claim I owe.

I am sending this letter via certified mail with a return receipt request as verification that the letter was sent and received.  I hope that you will comply with my request to cease and desist communication.  Should you continue to call or send mail to me, I will have no choice but to file a complaint with the Federal Trade Commission.

Any assistance you can give me with carrying out this letter of request will be appreciated.  I thank you in advance.

Sincerely,


<Your Name>
<Address>
<City, State, Zip Code>

**(Note:   Send this letter asking for a Cease and Desist by Certified Mail with a return receipt requested)**

## Section 7 – Bankruptcy a Last Resort

Sections one through six, I showed you how credit agencies work, the difference of a credit report and credit score. I gave you ways to contact credit agencies to get FREE copies of your reports, writing letters to dispute errors, how to communicate with your creditors and debt collectors and lastly your RIGHTS as a consumer.

Section three I gave you steps on what bills to gather, how to create a debtor's and household expense sheets. You can't begin a debt management program without first knowing how much debt you owe and to whom it is owed. You also need to know what income is coming in and the expenses you are paying out. This data is important to know in order to set up a payment schedule or ways to reduce your expenses. Once you have the information at hand you are ready to start your debt management program.

Upon writing letters to get your three credit reports, compare your credit reports with your debtor's list and looking for errors; you have taken your first step. If any errors are found you must write letters to the credit agencies to request corrections. If any accounts are past the Statute of Limitations (SOL) request that they be removed. The same applies to any hard inquiries (credit checks) that are past the two year limit. You should receive an updated credit report with a letter showing what changes were or were not made to your credit report. If you still feel an account is stilling showing an incorrect status; you will need to write directly to the creditor to see if they will send the correct information.

Lastly, after contacting the credit agencies, your creditors and dealing with any debt collectors you should have handled your debts. Were you able to get updated credit reports, made payment arrangements with your creditors, able to get accounts removed due to SOL, got debt collectors to stop contacting you? If so, you are on your way to managing your debt as you follow your plan. While in time by following the five ways to improve your credit report; you should see an increase in your credit score within six to twelve months.

Now there is another scenario that you must take into consideration. After going through all the above and you learn that your debt limit is too much for you to create a debt management plan; your income was just not enough to allow you extra to pay

debts; or you are under employed or unemployed. You've tried to

find a second job, reducing expenses, moving to a smaller place or

in with a relative, tried to get creditors to work with you, but you

find you're at the end of your rope and the creditors and/or debts

calls start again. They are driving you up the wall and there is

nothing you can do toward paying your debts. Wait, this leaves

another alternative to consider. **BANKRUPTCY**! Something you

tried to **AVOID**.

To some BANKRUPTCY is a stigma, dirty word, or

however you choose to label it. Yet it is not either of the above. It

is an alternative means to help you as a consumer get a FRESH

start. You've tried to find ways to pay off your debts but you see

no way clear to do so. It will mess up your credit report, sure it will,

but isn't it already in poor shape? Filing a bankruptcy will

definitely be a big decrease to your credit score. It will for a while

keep you from obtaining credit. However, if your credit is so bad

that you even need to consider bankruptcy, then you weren't able to

get any more credit anyhow. You have to consider your financial situation and future plans. If you have to file bankruptcy, then do so, rid your debt, and begin to work on rebuilding your credit. In time, you will get new credit and the bankruptcy will age off your credit report once you prove your credit worthiness.

First you need to understand the different bankruptcy plans available to you; the qualifications and which will benefit you. Plus every consumer's financial circumstances are different. There are those that are deeply in debt, those with moderate debt and some with smaller debts. Choosing to file a bankruptcy also depends on whether you are employed or unemployed. Chapter 7 (Liquidation) rids you of all your personal unsecured debt (credit cards, medical bills, etc.), you might lose your car or home but in some cases you won't. Chapter 13 (wage earner plan) you are allowed to repay some debt minus the interest. Chapter 11 (business re-organization) allowing an individual operating his business (sole proprietorship) or a large business can file bankruptcy and still operate while paying its debt. All these are under the supervision of the federal courts.

**Chapter 7 (Liquidation):** this bankruptcy can remain on your credit report for ten years. You can't include some taxes, alimony or child support, or student loans. Students getting an administrative loan discharge through the Department of Education or income-based repayment plan before trying to discharge the debt from bankruptcy first. After attempting to pay it might show a hardship and the judge may consider loan for discharge; mainly those 60 years of age have a better success rate (Powell. April 2016). There are times your car can be excluded if it is needed for getting to work and your home if you have no place to live. All these depend on the individual's circumstances and the judge handling the case. The bankruptcy code is complex and you will need a lawyer on your side.

Another thing a Chapter 7 has to be paid for up-front. The costs of filing and attorney's fees can be from $1,250 and more. So if you are planning to go this route you should start saving if you don't already have the funds. Plus you have to present documents to the court about your income/expenses, debts and amount owed, tax records, bank account, assets, etc. Before the filing you will need to attend a credit counseling class and another after the case has been heard by the courts. If your case is approved by the courts you will receive a letter of discharge.

**Chapter 13 (Wage Earner Plan):** you must be employed to be allowed to file Chapter 13. You will need enough income to cover a reorganize debt plan per the bankruptcy provisions. If your house is in foreclosure filing a Chapter 13 will put such proceedings on hold. However, you will need to keep your mortgage current. Thus, if you are behind on your payments filing a Chapter 13 will give you an opportunity to pay the back payments. You also will have the opportunity to pay off your debt within 3 to 5 years. This is the usual time a court gives an individual to settle a Chapter 13 case. You only need the court filing fees up front so your lawyer can file your case. Once your case is filed you no longer have to pay toward your debt or speak to your creditors. Should a creditor calls simply say you have filed a Chapter 13 and give them your lawyer's information. DO NOT discuss your debt with your creditor or any debt collector.

When filing a Chapter 13 you may be required to send to the trustee the monthly amount of your Chapter 13 plan while the case is pending in court. The amount of your monthly payment for your wage earner plan is determined from what is left after your expenses are deducted from your income sheet. **Note: If your income after expenses shows you do not have enough to support a wage earner plan; you may be advised to file a Chapter 7 instead.** Once your wage earner plan is approved the amount you sent in is applied to the plan. Your lawyer's fees are included in the plan and he/she is one of the debts that is paid first. Thus a Chapter 13 filing allows an individual the chance to pay off their debts and reorganize their finances over 5 years' time.

Be mindful that if you don't keep your Chapter 13 (wage earner plan) payments current and your case is dismissed; your creditors will begin to come after you. There are times within a limited time, if you catch up your back payments, your case could be reinstated. Your lawyer would be the best person to let you know in this case. It would be in your best interest to try and stay current with your Chapter 13 case.

**Chapter 11 (Business Organization):** this type of bankruptcy is usually used by businesses than individuals. It gives a business time to reorganize and service their customers while they are paying down their debts. These debts can have a payment plan, have time extended to pay, or even have the debt reduced. A trustee appointed by the U.S. court will supervise and work with the business until the debt is paid off. The trustee will report to the courts, review the business operations/finances till the Chapter 11 is completed.

Filing a bankruptcy can be a financial blow to your credit report and decrease your credit score; but its purpose is to give consumers who have tried to get out of debt an opportunity to do so and start over. The main objective is to enable individuals to become debt free and manage their future finances. It is up to the individual to not get back in the same situation after they have taken advantage of a Chapter 7 or Chapter 13. Also, when you file a bankruptcy, you can't file again until the 10 year reporting time has lapsed. Remember BANKRUPTCY helps you to gain debt freedom; but it doesn't teach you how to remain that way.

## Summing it Up for You

You read in Section  about bankruptcy and how it can affect your credit report.  I also gave you some details about each type of bankruptcy available to you.  Many individuals knew how a bankruptcy will affect their credit but many didn't understand how they worked.  After reviewing the above section I hope I helped you to understand their process.  Chapter 7 and Chapter 13 are available to help individuals to get out of debt.  If you are deeply in debt and find yourself with no way out, bankruptcy may be your alternative.

You will need to contact a lawyer who deals with bankruptcy cases.  They can go over your financial circumstances with you and be able to help you decide if bankruptcy is for you.  If you know that your only way out of debt is by filing a Chapter 7, be prepared to discuss the costs for filing and the lawyer's fees.  It would be best to know this before you go to his/her office with your documents.  When filing either bankruptcy plan your lawyer will give you a list of all the documents you will need to bring.  The sooner you deliver all the documentation the sooner your lawyer will be able to determine which bankruptcy to file.

A Chapter 7 filing costs money up front in full before a lawyer will file your case. Some will work out a plan pay in installments till you reach the amount needed. A Chapter 13 filing most lawyers will want a filing fee and a small down payment or not because their fee is included in the Chapter 13 case plan. You do need to be employed to be eligible to file this bankruptcy plan. Be sure to use a lawyer that has experience with bankruptcy proceedings, it will help your filing to go smoothly. Bankruptcy codes are complex and not every lawyer is familiar with them. I can't stress this enough about selecting the right lawyer to handle your bankruptcy filing. You can bounce back from bankruptcy. It is not the end but a new beginning.

# Section 8 – Staying Debt Free and Increasing Credit Score

We're nearly done after completing the other sections we turn to ways to stay out of debt and to manage our finances. While managing debt and maintaining your credit report; you will see your credit score increase. Let's take a look at how you can give your credit score a lift up. Paying off the following bill payoffs would be a helpful start:

**Make Payments on Time:** making your payments on time is the best thing you can do to help increase your credit score. Paying on time and not missing payments are viewed by the credit bureaus more favorably than any other factor.

**Highest Interest Rate Debts:** high credit card interest rates cause you to have a more debt. Paying these cards off first reduces your debt risk and increases your credit score gradually.

**Credit Cards with Lowest Credit Limits:** credit bureaus analyze your total debt so try to keep credit card limit low in regards to your credit card limit. If the credit card with the lower limit is near its maximum; pay it off first.

**Keep Your Credit Utilization Under 30%:** try not to charge up to the limit on any credit card or account limit. If you have high revolving balances where you are using more than 30% of your available credit; then it becomes an issue that will negatively affect your credit score. It is a good idea to keep your borrowing less than a third of what you are allowed. Doing so you will see improvement in your credit utilization.

**Student Loans:** paying off your student loans helps to reduce your debt-to-income ratio which can be a good thing. However, having a long record of paying on time will help your score. If you have no other installment loans (student loans are considered installment loans); paying it off could affect your debt mix. Credit cards are revolving debt; credit bureaus like to see a mixture of both types of debt in your report. Stretching out payments on a student can be a good thing in this case.

Oh, one other way of relieving student loan debt until you become able to pay on it is to enroll in an Income Driven

Repayment Plan (**IDRP**). It is a plan that goes by your income and determines if you can or cannot pay your student loan(s). A IDRP should be taken into consideration if you are on a fixed income. It would be a good idea to check with your student loan servicer provider. They would be able to tell you if you qualify for the plan. Good Luck.

**Past Due Bills:** it is better to pay back what you owe on debts that are very late. It will increase your credit score a lot, but not right away. Lenders want to see that you paid back debts you owed. You may want to pay recent past due bills first.

Remember having a good or better credit score is essential to your financial planning. Unless you are able to pay cash for everything you need to establish a good credit report and maintain a high credit score; to live a quality life style. Some seniors feel their credit score is no longer important to them. Wrong! Seniors still need to maintain a good credit score for it is viewed by landlords when trying to rent an apartment. Lenders view it if you are purchasing a smaller home and some financial institutions view credit reports.

Did you know that paying down your debt is a good investment? It can improve your net worth and give you other benefits. Below are some ways that paying down your debt can change your life to benefit you:

**Receive an Instant Return on Your Money:** think of all those high interest rated credit cards hitting on an average APR of 14% or higher. Paying off any high interest debt (credit cards, payday loans, etc.) will give you an instant return on your money. Simply not having to pay those high monthly payments will put more money back into your pockets.

**Cash Flow Improvement:** you will notice that you are having more money leftover at the end of each month. You'll be able to put money into a savings account or add more to other bill payments to clear remaining debts. Perhaps you'll be able to invest in taxable accounts or save for retirement. As you are making progress, you will see extra cash flow improvements.

**Having Financial Freedom:** paying off debt can reduce your monthly expenses when you no longer have debt burdens. You escape the feeling of living paycheck to paycheck as you struggle to get by each week. As long as you keep earning an income you can afford your monthly obligations. When you no longer owe debts each month you can think about other things like; working less, opening a business, switching jobs or even taking a decent vacation.

## Summing It Up for You

This section talked about ways to stay debt free which would help to increase your credit score. Once being debt free you may find that the urge to start spending creeps back upon you. I know the feeling for at first I wanted to start buying things again. I had to let my thoughts drift toward saving and sticking to ways to keep from getting into debt again. Thus the steps listed in Section 8 were my guide to keeping me out of debt. These same steps can be your guide to staying out of debt.

Like me, you have to resist the urge to start buying or opening more credit accounts. It can be hard but it can be accomplished once the feeling of being debt free sets in. You've gotten out of debt and you can see your credit score slowly rising. The idea is not to get roped into building up new debt. You can start looking at creating new spending habits, saving more and even living a simpler lifestyle. The stress of having a lot of debt to deal with is no longer a burden to you. You can now begin to manage your finances and enjoy a debt free life.

Like me, I was able to control my spending and in doing so, I had more money left to begin saving and enjoy some of my earnings. After reading this section I'm hoping you will have found ways to help you manage your new found freedom from debt. Now you can read on about living a stress free life with less as I have.

## Section 9 – Living Stress Free on Less

Congratulations, we've come through the major steps in becoming debt free and on your way to increasing your credit score. What a great feeling to have worked through getting ourselves out of debt. You've managed to eliminate a great amount of stress from your life; now it is time to work toward managing your finances. You do this by saving, budgeting, and utilizing extra money that comes from other sources. The unexpected money that appears out of nowhere, you can use instead of dipping into your budget.

Unexpected money can be: change or a $10 bill you find in a piece of clothing just as you are about to wash it; or a class action settlement or rebate check you forgot about. Other sources could be money from a yard sale, side jobs (shoveling snow, cutting lawns, child care, etc.) These small amounts of money come in handy to help pay toward bills, saving or even taking that long awaited vacation. Some other ideas you can use to keep from letting this new money go to waste are:

- **Paying extra toward a loan that you want to pay off early**
- **Creating an emergency fund**
- **Use it to help pay down other debt each month**
- **Add it to your savings account**

The main thing is not to keep it lying around or in your pocket making it available for spending. Utilizing store or restaurant coupons to save and then put the savings into a jar to be later put into your bank's savings account. When creating an emergency fund try to save at least six to eight months' worth of bills and household expenses. It wouldn't take much for an emergency to hit that would cause you to start using your credit cards. It could quickly put you back into debt. Getting overwhelmed with debt would bring on stress which you're trying to avoid.

Now that your debt is under control you may want to think about what you plan to do next. By having all the previous debt may have caused you to delay attending school to further your career, changing jobs, taking that vacation, or buying your first house. Being debt-free may give you the opportunity to now change jobs or buy that new car. You worked hard to get out or debt and sacrificed much.

Like you, I had to come to terms with making better financial decisions if I were to stay debt free. It can be tempting to want to spend your available money but it would not be a smart financial decision. It would be better to find ways to invest it (start a small business, savings and that emergency fund). It would be a good idea to have a budget set up that would show you where you are spending your money. It's best to be sure you have some savings and an emergency fund available. Making good financial decisions regularly will enable you to remain debt free.

Good financial decisions, budgeting and spending less will also keep your life stress free. When you aren't loaded down with debt and under stress you feel better and your mind is open to put some fun into your life. You can now think about taking a vacation with the family, spend more time with the kids or even buy that big purchase you have been putting off. You deserve some relaxation and enjoyment after all your hard work. Reward yourself before you get back into managing your future bills and increasing your credit score.

When making those financial decisions look for ways to cut back on spending. Try and find more of the simple things to enjoy in life. Remember the things you did before you got into debt that probably didn't cost much or were free. The simple things we did that brought joy and happiness in our life. They didn't cost a lot of money but just more of our time. Life was even less stressful before we got to overspending and getting into debt. Try putting more fun into your life and spending less. Live a simpler lifestyle, make better financial decisions, spend less and continue to manage any debt and watch your credit score increase.

Looking back over all you've learned from your Self-Help Guide and accomplished; you can say you've come a long way. It took a while to achieve your goal. The objective now is to keep in control of your debt and spending; while you manage your finances. This will help your credit reports to improve and your credit score to increase. Guess what?

Congratulations, you **DID IT YOURSELF!**

## Summing It Up for You

Wow! We've completed Your Self Guide to Debt and Credit Management book with the conclusion of this session 9. You are on your way to being debt-free and increasing your credit score. You started with the first section which helped you to get to know your credit reporting agencies. Other sections instructed you how to get started, what documents that were needed, where to send letters, and how to go about getting in control of your debt.

I'm sure at first it seemed like a big task but later you may have found that the majority of the work dealt with time. There was the period of sending for your credit reports, waiting for their return, comparing them to each other and your creditor's list. Again, sending out more letters to have corrections or accounts removed from credit reports, waiting again for responses. Now writing to your creditors, collection companies, etc. and waiting for their responses. It was all so very time consuming but necessary in order to properly have the correct documentation.

I would hope that all those who have read this book learned

quite a bit about how credit works. Also, the ways you have available to work with the credit agencies and creditors to get your credit reports updated. The book also was written to help others know their rights and those of creditors and collection companies. By knowing your rights and how to fight for them helps to eliminate some of the fear that some have of the credit system. If you are well organized, have all your documentation, know what can be expected, and whom to contact, you can manage your debt problem yourself. You just need to be prepared for all the time between letters written and responses. Patience is definitely a quality you need during your work.

The sections were written to easily guide you through the steps needed to complete them. Sample forms and letters were given that have proven to get responses and that could be easily made to suite each individual's situation. I've used them and from my experience they are suitable for their purpose. The forms in Section 5 dealing with the Statute of Limitations (**SOL**) are samples of **WI, IL & IN**. However, you can search on the Internet for a copy of your state's Statute of Limitation's document. It would be good to have a copy of your state's **SOL** for your

information. Once you have this information it will help you to

note any credit account that is past the Statute of Limitations.

After checking your credit reports and locating any **SOL**

accounts you can send out the required letter(s) to have them

removed. This self-help guide is meant to help those that are

having debt problems. I feel and hope the steps were easy to follow

and the information understandable. A person can get a bit

discouraged at times when waiting on responses from the credit

agency or creditor. **DON'T!** If you are serious about getting out of

debt and in control of your finances; then you must have

**PATIENCE**. It will be worth your while to continue on your

course to becoming **DEBT-FREE**! Believe me, I struggle more

than once with debt problems and completed the process of

becoming debt-free. Yet, being human, I slipped back into debt

but I knew how to get myself back out.

You can use this self-help guide more than once and even

use it to help others that may be struggling with debt. There is

updated information included for which I referenced at the end of the book. However, the majority of the book is written from proven experience and factual information that will enable you to become debt-free. Once you get serious about tackling your debt problem this self-help guide will help you achieve your goal. It also has some tips on staying out of debt and ways to generate extra income. Becoming debt-free and not having the stress associated with it; will leave you free to pursue a new job, further your education, buy that new car or house, save for your kids college, save more, create that emergency fund and save for your kids college education.

Section 9 lists some money saving tips, uses for unexpected money and just having fun. A few more ways to generate extra cash would be:

- **Sell items on Craig's List or eBay.**
- **Do Survey's over the Internet and get paid**
- **Transfer credit cards to a lower interest card**
- **Hold a garage sale**

These are just a few ways but you may have other opinions or thoughts on the subject. This self-help guide is loaded with good, proven ways to work toward improving your credit,

updating your credit reports, and dealing with your creditors and

Collection Company, crediting a creditor list, budget, and

eliminating your debt. Writing this self-help guide is my way of

sharing my experience with you. While guiding you through how

I accomplished becoming debt-free. It wasn't easy but I was

determined to get back in control of my finances, rebuild my

credit report and increase my score.

The debt problem is real and a big struggle for many

consumers to deal with over time. I know that those who purchase

this self-help guide; uses it will be glad they did. Becoming debt-

free will take work but the rewards are worth your time. You took

the first step by purchasing this self-help guide. What are you

waiting for go get **STARTED** toward **YOUR DEBT-FREE LIFE!**

# Financial Terms that May Be Helpful to Know

**ACH Authorization:** This lets you have your bill payments taken out of your bank account to pay your bills automatically each month. It guarantees your payments will be paid on time per the date you select to have the money taken out of your account. You usually sign an ACH authorization form for the creditor you want to pay. Remember: the creditor will take the FULL payment amount out. So be sure you wish to have automatic payments taken out for your bill payment.

**Agreement/Contract:** These legal documents make a loan official. These documents show the terms of the loan between you and the lender. Once you sign the loan agreement/contract you are legally responsible for paying back the money and any added interest or fees.

**APR:** The (Annual Percentage Rate) which is the interest payable on the money you borrowed plus other fees shown as annual rate of charge.

**Arrears:** When you miss any installment payments you are said to be in arrears (behind). The same is for payments overdue. When you get behind or miss payments it can affect your credit score. Try to pay your debt payments on time.

**Assets**: These are anything you own that has financial value. The cash in your bank accounts, stocks/bonds, whole life insurance policies, home, car and other items that a creditor decides is an asset. Whenever you apply for government programs they usually count your assets as income that can easily put you over the income qualifying for the minimum.

**Balance:** This can be the amount you own on a loan, mortgage, to a creditor or even the money in your bank account.

**Bounced Check:** A check" bounces" when your bank account doesn't have enough money to cover the check. The bank will return the check marked unpaid and charge you a returned check fee and possibly an overdraft fee. (See NSF later in this list)

**Budget:** A budget can help you keep track of your spending and expenses. You will be able to see where your money goes and how it's spent.  Income (money coming in) and expenses (money paid out) such as groceries, rent, gas, utilities, bills, etc.)

**Cash Advance:**  Money given to you against a prearranged line of credit such as credit card, loan agreement.  It also applies to small loans provided by payday loan companies.

**Charges:** These amounts can be what financial companies charge you for using their services.as a customer.  Such fees can be ATM fees, teller fees, interest, cash advances charges, money order/certified check fees, etc.  They can also charge you for overdraft fees, returned check fees, late payment fees, stop-payment fees, etc.

**Credit Bureau:**  A credit reporting agency that collects data from companies and other sources and provides this information on individual consumers.  Lenders use this information to get your credit rating and see how responsible you are at paying your bills.  Landlords and some employers are beginning to use credit bureaus to check on consumers.  There are three main credit bureaus that provide this data: **TransUnion, Experian and Equifax.**

**Credit Report:** A document that contains your credit history including data from banks, mortgage companies, retailers and collection agencies. It also can show bankruptcies, judgements, tax liens, and your handling of your bill payments. It would be good to get your free copy of your credit report from each of the three agencies once a year to check their accuracy.

**Credit Score:** A number that creditors look at to determine if you are someone that will pay your bills. Credit agencies determine this number by how you manage your credit based on five categories. They are your: Payment History (35%); Outstanding Debt (30%); Length of Credit History (15%); New Credit Pursuit (10%); and Credit Mix (10%).

**Debt:** Money you owe to an individual, company or the government.

**Debt-to-Income Ratio (DTI):** the personal finance measure that compares the amount of debt you have to your total income. It is used by lenders to measure your ability to handle your payments each month and repay the money you borrowed.

**Early Repayment:** You paid back a loan or debt before the arranged due date. Some banks and companies charge fees for this but many do not. Example: If you have a loan, mortgage, payday loan, etc. and the payment arrangement is for 1, 2 or 3 years. Yet you pay the full debt off before 1, 2 or 3 years you will have paid off the debt early and saved yourself a lot on interest. This is why if you can pay $5 or more over the minimum due monthly you would save on interest and pay off your balance early.

**Fixed-Rate Interest:** Rate that stays the same through the entire loan term.

**Gross Income:** The amount your employer pays you before taxes, insurance, retirement contributions (IRA or 401K), and other withholdings are deducted.

**Interest:** Can be understood in two ways: as the amount you earn on saving/checking accounts and investments or it also the interest you pay on money you borrow known as the percentage. It is included in the total cost of a loan (APR).

**Loan:** Money you borrow with the understanding that it is to be paid back per the agreement that you legally signed.

**Loan Term/Loan Period:** The length of time you borrow the money. It can range from a week, month or years. This depends on the terms shown in the loan agreement or contract.

**Net Income:** Employee's "take home pay" or the amount left over after deductions are taken out of their pay check.

**NSF**: means Non-Sufficient Funds which says you did not have the money in your account to cover a check. Usually your bank or credit union will charge you a fee if this happens. Some will also want to charge you a returned check fee too. You do have a right to challenge to get

these fees overturned. Try speaking to the bank or credit union manager. Good Luck with that.

**Online Banking:** You can go online (Internet) or to the web page of your bank/credit union and do your banking services that way. You can check your balances, order checks, pay bills, make transfers and do many other services.

**Outstanding Balance:** The amount of money left to pay on a loan, mortgage or other bill account.

**Payday Loan/Payday Advance:** Short term loans that can be used for emergency expenses until you get paid. They charge large fixed rate fees on the amount borrowed and you have till your next payday to pay it off. Now they do allow you an opportunity to extend the loan. This however, will take you longer to pay off the loan and your interest builds up. It would be better to pay whatever you can over the regular payment amount to decrease the interest and pay the loan off faster. These loans are available to individuals that cannot obtain credit elsewhere.

**Penalty Charges:** Charges that you pay if you are late on your payments, have bounced checks, broken your loan agreement and NSF.

**Rate:** The fee a lender or creditor charges an individual on a loan agreement or contract as an Annual Percentage Rate (APR).

**Transaction:** The movement of money. When withdrawing cash from your banking or credit union account, that is a transaction. When making a payment on a debt, that is a transaction.

**Underpayment**: A loan payment that is less than what you are required to pay on a certain date.

Perhaps these explanations of common financial terms will help you to understand some of the language used by professionals in the business world. I felt that these are the ones that you may have heard or seen in past business dealings the most. You won't feel so intimidated when discussing business matters. Being familiar with the business language will give you more confidence. So brush-up on these financial terms before you begin writing your letters.

# REFERENCE

Richmond, S., March 6, 2015. What Affects Your Credit Score? Retrieved from

www.Investopedia.com/articless/personalfinance

Http:www.consumer.FTC.gov/articles/0058-creditrepair. (2013)

Weston, L. March 20, 2016. Money Talk; How to deal with debt collectors. Retrieved from

www.latimes.com/business/la-Fi-montalk-20160320-column.html

Brinkley-Budget, C. March 25, 2016. 5 Random reasons your credit score could go up. Retrieved from:

www.yahoo.com/finance/news/5-random-reasons-crredit-score-160000915.html

Clements, N. March 25, 2016. The risk and rewards of consolidating credit card debt. Retrieved from:

www.Forbes.com/sites/nickclements/2016/03/25/the

-risks-and-rewards-of-consolidating-credit-card-

debt/#56bc63

Experian. April 7, 2016. A personal credit report.

Retrieved from: www.Experian.com/view.

Powell, Farrant. April 27, 2016. Discharge of Student Debt

Possible During Bankruptcy. Retrieved from:

www.USnews.com/education/best-colleges/paying-

for-college/articles/2016-ov-26/discharge-of-

student-debt-possible

Pecha, Aimee. July 29, 2016. 5 things debt collectors will

no longer be able to do to you. Retrieved from:

www.CBSnews.com/news - money watch

www.ingramcontent.com/pod-product-compliance
Lightning Source LLC
Chambersburg PA
CBHW070030210526
45170CB00012B/529